SEASONS

Taniya Senanayake

BookLeaf Publishing

India | USA | UK

Presentation by *BookLeaf Publishing*

Web: www.bookleafpub.com

E-mail: info@bookleafpub.com

ISBN : 9789357612418

First edition 2021

DEDICATION

To my Grandma and Grandpa, who both always loved and nurtured my passion for writing. This one's for you Achchiamma and Seeya.

PREFACE

Dear Reader,

Welcome to the hidden chapters of my life. Come and join me on this journey as I navigate my adolescent years and the challenges and triumphs I have faced during this season. Although many of these moments are drawn from my own personal experiences, I hope you know that they are not only mine and that they could be yours too. My one desire for you, is that as I bare my heart in writing, you are able to relate intimately with my words and come to your own sense of tranquillity and understanding of yourself, the world around you and this season you are in.

Keep your head up
~ Taniya

Seeking Freedom

Speeding down the highway, without a care in
the world.
Feeling the summer breeze rushing through my
hair,
As the golden sun bows down, drawing the
evening to an end.
The blaring music drowns out all my thoughts.
The thoughts that are keeping me up at night,
Like monsters hiding under my bed, only in my
mind.
But I know that you are gone and I need to find
my peace.
So, I'm speeding down the highway to a place,
Where I can forget and be free.

Nostalgia

When I think about it,
Over the years as it passes by.
I miss the warm water and the soft sand.
I miss the freedom and tranquillity,
Of the atmosphere of this place.
A place where I could forget and be me,
With the people I love and love me.
Where every day was different and new,
Everyday had an exciting adventure awaiting
me.
But as I sit here, displeased with my life,
My heart hurts with this nostalgia, wanting to go
back.
Back to safety, my place where I desire to be so
dearly.

2:03am

It's 2:03,
And I can barely sleep.
I'm just thinking of what this world could be.
If only we all showed a bit of care and
sensitivity,
It would make this journey the slightest bit more
easy.
But honestly, I just can't see,
Right now this idea, becoming a reality.
Seeing this world that we're in, split between
wealth and money.
By racism, hate and all types of inequalities,
And this is what it is - precisely.
So let's take a step and try to see,
We can make a change... I know for sure.
We can only hope for the next generation, that
they have a chance to be free.
To grow and love as we hope it to be.
Now I ask myself, could this just be a dream?
But time has ticked by and it's 2:14.
So maybe this is why I'm finding it hard to
sleep,
Knowing that more could be done by us as a
community.

Solidarity

To the women who laid out our foundations,
We say thank you for all you have fought.
For the battles and struggles you have endured,
So, equality and justice can be brought forth.

To the young girls and women, I stand with
today.
It is our time to build from the foundations that
have been laid.
In unity we shall stand towards the challenges
and inequity,
And uphold the fight for our impartial justice.

To the children of the future, the ones unborn,
We hope that there is no battle for your
generation to be fought.
That both men and women will be equal as one,
And that this long journey of independence has
found its worth and been won.

What Matters

It's now 9:23,
And I wonder if my mum still thinks I'm asleep.
But the reality is that I'm in a clinic, where the
air is so sterile and clean.
Much like a hospital, but a lot more
heartbreaking.
I watch as the morning sun invades through the
glass, past the street signs and trees.
Beating down on my friend, whose traumas
can't leave her at peace.
What matters to me, is that my friend has to be
in this room so helplessly.
She was taken advantage of by her boyfriend at
the age of 16,
And we're trying to see
If she can abort this horrific reminder of her first
pregnancy.

It's December 7,
And the trees at night make human-like shadows
and impressions.
I'm walking to my car at 10 past 11,
But the streetlights don't seem as bright in this
part of Melbourne.

Every car that passes by floods me with
emotion,
Will it slow down? Will someone get out?
It causes so much unnecessary commotion.
This 10-minute walk feels like an hour and it's
torturing.
But what matters to me is that for my own
safety,
I feel the need to clench my hand around my
keys,
Or feel like I need to be on my phone talking
Because walking alone at night doesn't feel safe
anymore to me.

It's 2019,
And this is no made-up story.
She sat me down with a tear welling in her eye,
A tear holding much pain and hurt, I could hear
her silent cry.
She was held captive by the secrets she faced
most nights.
When her once beloved spouse started
threatening her life.
Started cutting her off and making her doubt
everything in mind.
She begged me not to tell anyone as her voice
shook deep inside.
What matters to me is that women like her are
placed in the hardest cases.

That now the most dangerous places,
Were once the ones that made them feel the
safest.
Leaving them with gut-wrenching emotion and
unfamiliar faces.

In 20-whatever it may be,
I want my baby girl to grow up where she can
truly be free.
To grow, and thrive, and love as we hope to one
day see.
I want her to know that she is not controlled by
this patriarchy.
Better still, that something like that doesn't even
exist in her time and reality.
What matters to me is that I want to be in a
lifetime where we all have equal opportunities.
Where women have the same unspoken rights
and respect they need.
That my daughter doesn't have to feel unsafe
walking down the street.
That she won't have to face our time of social
hypocrisy.

That is what matters to me.

Frozen Roses

I want you to miss me like
The frozen roses miss the summer sun,
As winter's breath chills them at night.

I want all the memories to come flooding back
When all your mind wants to do is forget,
'Till all the love and life you had with me aches
to come back.

I want you to know that this right here is what I
feel
And I don't deserve to have the weight of the
world upon me.
For you were my world and I want you to realise
What this hell you have caused really feels like
to me.

Hope

As Dickinson once wrote - Hope is a thing with
feathers that perches in the soul.
But what happens when we hold onto that Hope
like it is dear life?
Clutching it ever so tightly with both hands.
And as we hold onto it, we end up crushing it
with our grip.
Crumbling to dust, seeping through our fingers
leaving us with nothing.
So what do we do next, when that Hope we
depended upon vanishes with the wind,
Dancing away like a distant dream or a
childhood memory.
So yes, Hope is a thing with feathers that
perches in the soul.
But once that feather disappears, our soul
realises that Hope is also just as dangerous
As the one thing we depended upon finds its
independence from us.

Childlike Naiveté

Who knew our innocents could be the line
between make believe and reality?
That our childlike naiveté would shelter our
world to give us a piece of sanity.
But when the truth is revealed, hitting the
ceiling,
And your world turns into something not so
appealing.
All that's left to do is realise that every moment
leading up to this has been nothing but a dream.
And one day, suddenly you're opening your eyes
to find everything is not simple and sweet.
That everything you once believed is all just past
reminiscent stories.
Yet even the ones you trust aren't heroes
anymore,
And there is not one person you should count
on.

Colour-blind

Do you remember when you saw the world in
colours?
When a vivid rainforest of tones exploded before
your eyes,
And the sun shone towards your face, so warm
and so bright.
The striking reflections of the lively lush green
envious trees,
Against the cool endlessness of the deep
glowing blue ocean,
Brought back the happiest memories of you
dancing in the sky as free as a bird.

Oh but then over time, the intensity of these
colours begin to fade.
Like a thick fog washing over the world as if it
were stuck in a haze, but only to you.
Or maybe someone has found a way to turn
down the saturation of your eyes,
Leaving everything looking as if it's stuck in this
lifeless emptiness.
And the happiness turns into a melancholic
loneliness,

As the memories vanished one by one into an
archived collection of monochromatic moments.

Little Grey Cloud

Is this it... is this what it feels like?
To be consumed by that little grey cloud that
constantly follows me around.
At times this grey cloud transforms into a dark
consuming storm
That sweeps me up in a moment, any moment.
It rapidly grows and grows, getting bigger and
bigger by the second.
Raining down on me as if Zeus himself
commanded this disaster
Upon my life.

I battle these lonely cold waves that crash over
me.
The stinging waters blind my sight,
Whilst drowning out the light,
As the shackled weights around my chest drag
me down beyond my might.
The water begins to make its way into my lungs
whilst I gasp for a breath.
As though there is nothing that can be done to be
saved for this death.

3 2 1, now I've gone under.

Submerged below the waves, in a chamber of
darkness.
Where the sounds of the world are completely
muted out
To nothing but a muffled hum, disorientating my
mind.
I try to swim up and grab hold of something,
anything.
But the rope around my wrists, tied around my
back make it almost impossible to break free
from,
Which only leaves me to sink like lead, further
and further into the trenches.

Suddenly, as if it were in a blink of an eye,
The waves reside and the storm subsides.
And that little grey cloud takes its place above
my head, in the sky.
Leaving me dripping wet and freezing cold,
with cuts and scars and as confused as ever.
Questioning whether this is real or will this
spontaneity last forever.

Safe Box

Sometimes I have these moments,
Where my head tells me it's game over.
That there is no one left in the world that would
care for me no longer.
This void of nothingness numbs me till I'm
freezing cold,
And I guess the bathroom floor just seems like
one of the only places for me.

I'm so exhausted from being stuck in this cycle
of self-annihilation.
Where I turn into this complete internal mess
and obliteration.
I'm held in this recurring limbo that seems
inescapable.
It's almost as if it's artificial yet it feels so
palpable.
I don't know, maybe I guess it's sort of habitual.

But I facade all of this with an unnatural
composure,
Through all this exposure,
That confines me in this hurt, feeling like
torture.
So I sit in this pain unable to gain any closure,

As to the world I'm just some put together
person in a poster.

So I suppress these moments in a safe box,
Since shoving it under the carpet won't hold and
won't do me any favours.
And I bury it six feet under, in the place that's
hidden away,
It's all I can physically do as I cannot speak
Of something so painful and God forsaken.

Minutes or Months

What do I do when I'm watching my whole
world explode around me?
When this fragile system that I kept in balance,
falls apart in a split second.
And there I am,
Just helplessly watching.

Just as a bird watches the petals fall one by one
from a rose,
So too do I.
Yet I am no bird. I am nothing.
I am just one amount of emptiness that is simply
existing.
Existing for the sake of those around me and not
for me.

Yet, as the distorted hums pierce my ears.
My mind cannot orientate this exact moment.
Or maybe this moment is a disjointed
accumulation of every moment?
And even the palpitation of my own heart,
Feels foreign to me and almost unwanted in this
moment.

I lay here, simply watching.

There is nothing I can do but let the numbness
wash over me,
Take hold of me,
Consume every single part of me.
As the one thing I depended on, ends up finding
its independence from me.

Brighter

Sometimes the world tends to get that little bit
more brighter.
A little less like a stranger or outsider.
Where my soul is heard and the weights seem
lighter,
And the troubles of my mind are dulled to a
notion that is minor.

Journey

Taking time to look around
As the years play in my mind.
Not to see how far I've come
But how far I've been brought.
It's been one hell of a journey
To get to a place of love and satisfaction.
From days where smiles hid my desperation.
But as the stars take their place in the night sky,
I realise that it was not my strength but
One from a place I couldn't reach alone.

One Step Closer

Sometimes I wonder as the autumn leaves fall,
And the restless wind howls amongst the trees,
Why do we fall in love with people we can't
reach?
Going through the crashing waves of emotions,
And treacherous night with no sleep and plenty
of tears,
All to realise it will never be anything we desire
to see.

But maybe we go through all this,
To precisely know and see that love exists for us.
And maybe our hearts require lessons and
mouldings to be the perfect fit,
For the one who was truly made for loving us.
So every heartache that we experience is one
step closer,
Closer to finding the one we will truly love.

Love

Love is what the heart calls a silent killer.
The more one experiences it, the more one falls
victim to it.
But love is not always a trap.
Sometimes it can sweep you off your feet to a
whole new place,
Changing the way you look at someone,
or even better, be the difference in this world.
Love is the most powerful emotion one can
possess.
It can break chains and built-up walls,
walls of isolation and despair.
Love can change someone's life.
Where there is fear and condemnation
and all else in the world fails,
Love will triumph over all.
One's love for another can be the key to their
heart.
It can inspire and motivate one's life and
purpose.
Love is all around us whether we realise it or
not;
From a parent to a child,
Through to a lifelong partnership.

Even though love is silent, it will speak louder
than all,
Infectiously spreading from the deepest crevices
of our heart.
For love is what we do not speak of but what we
truly feel.
Love is what this world of ours really needs.

Little Love

Just one thought had changed it all.
My heart felt something it had never felt before.
Simply knowing this was something I wanted.
This feeling was so safe and secure no matter
anything.
Looking at your unclear yet so beautiful face,
And holding your soft tiny hand in mine,
Makes the whole world seem just right.
I hope the time will come where I pass
something to you.
Something of me to my gorgeous future little
love.

Forbidden

I'd never known a forbidden love to exist until
our fated paths met.
It seemed like my Montagues were at war, once
more with your Capulets.
Although this time, it was not like the ancient
and literal sense.
But of one far more ignored, unspoken for and
complex.

Blue

I'd spend all my nights talking to you my dear.
Getting lost in your ocean blue eyes yet also
praying you were here,
As my mind dances to the perfect harmony of
your voice.
And oh in this moment all my heart can do is
rejoice,
Because you are perfection, from the little
dimples on your cheeks,
To the way your flawless smile forms and me
who it greets.
I'm surely not one to catch on to these types of
emotions,
But I suppose you have somehow got my heart
into full motion.

Beauty

You're the one I'd stay up all night with,
Huddled next to as the winter chill brings us
closer,
Watching the moon shining over the most
beautiful star next to me.
You shine so bright, the sun hides away in your
beauty,
Causing the whole world to stop and linger in
awe
Of you as you hold me tight, with a soft smile
and red nose.
I wonder as the shining stars and whispering
wind dance as one,
How was I so blessed to be graced by such a
diamond like you?

Months, Seasons, Changes

As the seasons change from one to another, there
is one thing that comes to mind.
One inconsistent constant that forever changed
my life.
I realise my dear, that it's you, I see in
everything around me.

From the endlessness of the oceans that are
reflected in your eyes,
To the perfect harmonies heard in every note you
speak.
It is no one but you I see in my future tree and
little ones.

And just as nature is blessed with the nurturing
of water,
So to, do you bless me with your presence,
Nurturing my edges and loving my fallen leaves.

Although, our seasons turned leaf by leaf, just as
the years themselves pass by,

It was through you I found the one thing I was in
search of,
And by the grace of God, you helped me find
my freedom.